EVERYDAY LEADERSHIP
By
Kent Myers

EVERYDAY LEADERSHIP
Copyright © 2022 by Kent Myers

CONTENTS

INTRODUCTION

The subject of leadership has been analyzed more often than almost any other in history. Over 20,000 books and untold thousands of articles have been written on the topic. Clearly, throughout the world, the concept of leadership is both timeless and intriguing.

Leadership can be a confusing subject. We have different—and at time, contrasting—theories of leadership (transactional, transformational, charismatic, and situational); varied different leadership styles (autocratic, authoritarian, pacesetting, democratic, coaching, affiliative and laissez-faire. Not to mention the many different attributes, skills and giftedness characteristics desired to be a great leader.

It can take so many different forms. It can take the form of a brash "command and control" style epitomized by General George S. Patton: *"Lead me, follow me, or get out of my way."*

Or it can take a subtler form of leadership as exemplified by Nelson Mandela: *"It is better to lead from behind and to put others in front, especially when you celebrate victory when nice things occur. You take the front line when there is danger. Then people will appreciate your leadership."*

President John F. Kennedy put it best when he observed, *"Leadership and learning are indispensable to each other."* Leaders learn to become leaders, and they continue to learn in their leadership roles.

I frequently get the opportunity to talk to different groups about leadership, and one of the first questions that I always enjoy asking is, *"How many of you, without question, unequivocally, would call yourself a leader?"* And it always generates an interesting response. Invariably, every single time, roughly one third of the audience will raise their hands. Of that third, half of them offer a tentative, half-a-hand raise, because they're not completely confident in that answer. And that's unfortunate because I think that we've elevated this term "leader" or "leadership" to something mysterious and unattainable.

Two other questions that I frequently ask are, *"What's the first attribute or word that you think of when you hear that word "leader" or "leadership?"* I get a variety of answers: "courage," "vision," "compassion," and "honesty." Finally, I ask: *"Who is the very first person that you think of when you hear those words, 'leader' or 'leadership?"* As with the previous questions, these answers vary, from that fifth-grade teacher to the wrestling coach to someone who sits atop the power hierarchy, like a president or a general.

Well, one thing that I know is true is that if 100

people are in a room and I ask the question: *"Give me your definition of leadership"*—I would probably get about 95 different answers. And that's because we all see leaders and leadership in slightly different ways.

I hope that after you navigate these pages, you will come to see leadership differently. I hope you see leadership not as a position or role that is reserved for the top echelon of the corporate organization chart, or for superheroes in heroic moments, but as *every one* of us *every day*. Interesting how the mention of the phrase "every day" resonates—how people interpret it—because they usually hear it one of two ways: Does an everyday kind of person mean *all of us*? And the other aspect is its chronology: *every single day.* This culmination of themes makes up an **Everyday Leader.**

Every one of us. Everyday.

An Everyday Leader is someone who thinks more about the needs of others than themselves, speaks with integrity, acts with purpose, and most importantly, one who consistently, positively impacts the lives of others every single day.

If you were to ask me the same question, *"Of whom do you think when you envision a true leader?"* I'd have to tell you a story—a story about one of the greatest jobs that I've ever had between my freshman and sophomore year in college, in a little town in the middle of Missouri. The job that I had was an umpire for a five and six-year-old T-ball league in the evenings. Now those of you that have ever been involved in five and six-year-old t-ball know that there are probably some great examples of leadership, and some not-so-great examples of leadership. But one night that I will always remember, I saw one of the greatest examples of an Everyday Leader that I've ever seen.

It was a July night; muggy, warm, dusty and the game had to be close to an end because we've been going for some time. Now to understand how five-and six-year-old t-ball works, is that kids rarely strike out in t-ball. So, what happens is one team will bat all the way around the order, and then it's the next team's turn, and they will bat all the way around the order. And after about an hour of play, the game is over. So, my job is really a glorified timekeeper.

On this night, a little boy was coming up to bat and he was the last batter for that team. As I glanced down and looked at my watch, I knew that there wasn't enough time for the next team to bat. I guessed that the parents felt the same, because behind me I could hear cooler lids shutting and people folding up their lawn chairs. Well as this little boy came up to bat, he had a big smile on his face and was just filled with joy. Now this little boy had unfortunately struck out twice that night. You see, this little boy had Down syndrome, so he struggled somewhat with muscle control.

He came up to bat, got up to the plate and stood in the batter's box. His coach came down off the first baseline. He helped him to spread his legs just right and to get his bat back up on his shoulder. I did my job and put the ball on the tee, and a little boy looks back at me and I kind of give him the confirming nod to go ahead. And that little boy swings as hard as he can and hits the tee and the ball falls off. And it's strike one.

Well, the coach comes over again, and gets him set up and gets his legs spread apart, and the bat up on his shoulder, and I put the ball on the tee, and the little boy swings as hard as he can and--!

He hits the tee again.

This time, that ball falls off the tee, directly in front of home plate. Well, no one possesses absolute knowledge on all of the rules of t-ball, so there's a moment of silence—what seemed like three minutes, but was likely only about three seconds.

And then that silence was broken by a voice from the opposing team's dugout. And all you could hear was, *"Run to first, run to first, run to first!"* And the little boy looks back at me, and I give him the universal sign 'run to first.' And he takes off as hard as he can toward first base, which is serendipitous because many try to run to *third*! And this little boy is going as hard as he can, and now at this time you see the opposing teams' coach, Coach Schuster, come out of the dugout, yelling for this little boy, cheering him. *"run the first, run to first".*

This little boy is more than halfway toward first base, when Coach Schuster turns to his catcher and screams, *"Throw the ball to first! Throw the ball to first!"* Well, if any of you understand the athletic ability of a five-year-old to make the throw from home plate to first base, you know what happens. It's not even close. It ends up on the far-right side of the base, with a whole bunch of little kids chasing after it. As that little boy rounds first base, Coach Schuster is now in the coaches' box cheering him on.

"Run to second! Run to second! Run to second!" And this boy is going as hard as he can, almost turning second base by the time that the other kids get to the ball.

Well, you can guess what happens. This little boy hits an inside-the-park homerun.

I get choked up telling that story because in my mind I can still see that little boy turning third base, running toward home with the biggest smile on his face and his arms pumping just as hard as they can. She stopped right before home plate, leaped and landed with both feet on home plate as I yelled SAFE!!! As loud as I could. You would have thought it was the seventh game of the World Series that had just been won. Kids from both teams met him, cheering. Every parent in the stand, regardless whose parent was for what kid, or for what team, they were all wildly applauding. It was one of those unbelievable, inspirational moments that I will remember all my life, because one man, in one moment, left the dugout and revealed his humanity.

That is always a great story, and a moment I will always remember. But a couple of years later, I was making my weekly call back home and talking to my parents. I was chatting with my mom, and I said, *"What happened in the little town of Boonville this week?"*

"Well," she said, *"we had the opportunity to go to Coach's funeral."* (I knew that Coach Schuster had passed away). I asked if the funeral was well attended? She told me that the church was full to its 200-seat capacity, but it still wasn't enough. 150 mourners had to stand outside.

We talk about Everyday Leadership, not in regard to hierarchy, or power, or authority, but to *character*. And that's exactly what Coach Larry was. He was a simple mechanic—one stall in a little garage taking care of people.

Well, the interesting thing about that service that my mom told me, was that there was a young man— probably in his early 30s at this point—who was now an executive for Special Olympics. That young man got up and delivered Larry's eulogy by telling the story of a night on a t-ball field when a coach changed the way that he saw himself, his very identity, and forever altered the trajectory of his life. One moment —one moment in time where one man decided to come emerge from a dugout, yet it irrevocably changed a young boy's life.

I've told that story hundreds, if not thousands of

times, and I'm sure that young man has, as well. It's what we might call the ripple effect in the legacy that Larry had, not because of his power or authority, not because of his position, but due to his **Everyday Leadership.**

Everyday Leaders positively impact the lives of people around them; not by their authority, but by the little things that they do with great love and kindness.

Everyday Leaders positively impact the lives of people around them; not by their authority, but by the little things that they do with great love and kindness.

I think about this impact in the from a recent family event. This past fourth of July weekend, my family were having dinner outside, and we had an uninvited visit from a small honeybee. My youngest daughter screamed in fear and waved her arms and the poor little bee flew away. I am sure we can all relate to that scene. We all may react a bit differently —some see a bee as a threat, others may see it as a nuisance; but few of us see that little bee as something very significant to our lives.

The reality is the honeybee is responsible for the pollination of nearly three quarters of the plants that produce 90% of the world's food. A third of the world's food production depends on bees. Put another way, for every third spoonful of food, we have the bees to thank for making it possible. Additionally, the honeybee pollinates 80% of all of the world's flowers. Seven years ago, Stanford University completed a study that found "If the honey bee ceased to exist, Mankind would be reduced to nearly a water-based diet." They concluded that "the honeybee is the most influential and significant species in our economy and ecology."

I am sure we ask ourselves, how can something so small and seemingly insignificant be so impactful? Unfortunately, I believe this may be the same way we see ourselves somedays. We may tell ourselves that we are not in a position to be significant or to impact the lives of others, but that, of course, is a fallacy. It is *not* our heroic efforts that make us significant in the lives of others—we are significant most often in the little things that we do: when we show someone compassion with a kind word; when we smile and brighten someone's day; when we tell someone that we appreciate them. It is in these little things that we all have the opportunity to be honeybees. We never know what someone else may be dealing with at any given moment, and how much a simple act of compassion might mean to them.

We have to remember, it's not the heroic moments

in life that have the greatest impact, in and with other people. It's the little things that we do that make the biggest differences. Just like Coach Larry coming out of that dugout, thereby changing the trajectory of that little boy's life. My challenge to you is just this: today and every day going forward, strive to become an Everyday Leader.

In the next few chapters, we are going to take a journey through eight commitments that Everyday Leaders make to themselves:

8 Commitments for Everyday Leaders

1. *Every day, I will demonstrate **kindness and caring** for all that I interact with.*

2. *Every day, I will **extend trust** even before it is earned and assume positive intent of everyone.*

3. *Every day, I will **be the example** that I want others to follow.*

4. *Every day, I will strive to make every person successful **through proactive accountability** and respect.*

5. *Every day, I will take **100% responsibility** of things within my control, **with zero excuses.***

6. *Every day, I will seek to **discover and develop potential** in everyone, including myself.*

7. *Every day, I will work for extraordinary results by focusing on* **our "why."**

8. *Every day, I will appreciate everything that I have and* **show gratitude** *to all while celebrating our progress.*

I understand that this is a different way to see leadership, but the reality is that when we change the way we see leadership, we change the way we see ourselves. When we change the way we see ourselves, we change the way that we see others. This perspective opens our eyes and allows us to see how we, in whatever role we play, can be significant in someone's life.

APPLICATION and DISCUSSION

- When you think of this definition of Everyday Leadership, who is the first person that comes to your mind and why?

- Of these eight commitments, which of them resonate most to you and why??

- What impact might a culture of Everyday Leadership have on an organization, a team, or a family?

COMMITMENT: What is one thing I can do *every day* to be better at Commitment One? Every day, I will demonstrate kindness and caring for all that I interact with?

1

COMMITMENT ONE

For many of you, I may be introducing you to a new way to look at leadership – a new perspective. I find the whole concept of perspective interesting. As leaders, co-workers, friends, and family members, we can find ourselves in a position in which we look at the *exact* same set of data and see completely different things. Let me give you a real example. Look at the sentence below and simply count every "F" in the following sentence:

**FINISHED FILES ARE THE RESULT OF
YEARS OF SCIENTIFIC STUDY COMBINED
WITH THE EXPERIENCE OF YEARS...**

Our brain processes this differently. It is yet another example of how we can see the same data but perceive things differently. How many "F"s did you see? Most people see four or five. Actually, there are six. No kidding, go back and look again. The reason is that the brain has difficulty processing the word "of."

While all of this may seem inconsequential, this exercise is an example of how we can see things differently, often creating miscommunication, and potentially missing opportunities.

The concept of Everyday Leadership is looking at things from a different perspective. The reality is that when we see *leadership* differently, we begin to see *ourselves* differently. We begin to see the influence and impact that we have in the little things we do. When we see ourselves differently, then we begin to see others differently. We begin to see who they are and what they need.

This is critical for Everyday Leaders in the pursuit of Commitment Number One: **Every day, I will demonstrate kindness and caring for all those with whom I interact.**

This commitment focuses on two impactful key words – kindness and caring. They may seem similar, but in fact, are quite different.

Caring is a *feeling* – something that exists in our heads and in our hearts. It is an inner experience. Caring happens when we see another person in need, and hurting in some way, and we desire to alleviate their suffering. Caring people acknowledge that all humans suffer.

Kindness is action oriented. It is at the core of many aspects of the definition of Everyday Leadership: An *everyday* leader is a person who *thinks* more about the needs of others than themselves, *speaks* with integrity and *acts* with purpose, consistently, positively impacting the lives of others *every day*.

Caring Changes our Mindset, Kindness Changes Lives.

Kindness and caring are a couple of words that get lumped together often, sometimes with other terms that we use to describe the same type of things: kindness and caring, empathy and sympathy, and compassion. As we think about putting these feelings in action, I want to elucidate on some of these nuances.

Empathy is the way that many of us feel when we see someone in need or who is hurting in some way – and we understand how they feel – we feel that we want to help them. We've all been in that position, with the intention of making their lives a little bit better. But the most interesting thing, and the most important, is what happens after we have that initial feeling, because there is one of two ways to go: despite the feeling, we take no action, which is complacency; or we act upon those feelings of sympathy and empathy to make them feel better. When we take action on our feelings, we demonstrate compassion. *Sympathy and empathy, without action, is just wasted compassion.* Everyday Leaders do their best never to miss an opportunity to change the life of another by demonstrating compassion.

When I think about true compassion—empathetically feeling others' needs and acting on it—I think about Mrs. Mayo, one of my neighbors when I was growing up who lived across the street. I got to know her because I mowed her yard; but I also got to know her because, for 39 years, Mrs. Mayo was a cafeteria lunch lady. She served food in an elementary school in the little town I grew up in. When I was in college, I spoke with my mom to find out all the events at home, and she mentioned that they had had the opportunity to go to Mrs. Mayo's retirement party. A retirement party for the cafeteria lunch lady? I thought that was interesting. A lot of stories were told, some of which my mom hadn't even known! One of those stories was that Mrs. Mayo knew the name of every child that went through those lines and strived to call them by name every single day – for 39 years! I thought that was amazing, but I didn't know why.

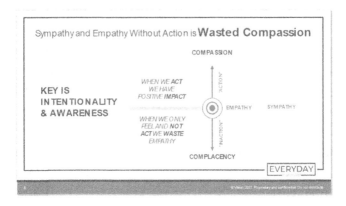

I must tell you, though—another reason that Mrs. Mayo is so near and dear in my memories, is that every Christmas Eve, she would bake our family a large batch of cinnamon rolls. And as long as I can remember, Mrs. Mayo's cinnamon rolls were our special Christmas morning extravagance from the neighbor across the street. As a kid, it was a tough dilemma on Christmas morning—do we run to all those presents waiting for us under the Christmas tree, or toward the wonderful aroma of cinnamon rolls coming from the oven! I remember being home for Christmas after college, and Mrs. Mayo called. *I have your cinnamon rolls ready but I'm just not feeling very well. Can somebody come over and pick them up?* So I went across the street—the place that I'd been many times, and knocked on the door. I had picked up enough manners by then to know that I couldn't just grab the cinnamon rolls and run, so I went inside to catch up and talk for a while.

As we sat down, I asked her, *I heard a story about you—that for all of those years that you served food to kids, you called them by name, every one of them, every day*. She paused, and looked at me and then said, *Yes, I did*. She said, *You need to understand that not every kid that came through the lunch line had a loving mother and a father, that they didn't have all of the things that you were given in life*. She said, *So I thought, there's not much I can do about that, but if I could learn their names and I could call them by their names when they came through the breakfast line in the morning, maybe it would start their day off right. And if I continued to do that when they came back for lunch, maybe I could keep their day going well*. Then she said something to me that I will never forget. She said, *I never saw my job as serving food; I saw my job as serving kids.*

What a blessing Mrs. Mayo was to every one of those lives that she touched. She was *sympathetic* in that she saw the need to acknowledge these kids, and she was *empathetic* that she understood that not all of these kids came from a solid family background and were probably struggling with things that she couldn't comprehend. But she didn't stop with just empathy; she did something about it – intentionally – for 39 years of her life. She demonstrated compassion every day by caring about those kids, calling them by name and trying to better their lives *every day*. When we think about the jobs that we do, we can view them from a number of perspectives. We can think that a job is a means to paycheck—an occupation—or we can think about it the 'Mrs. Mayo Way'—a calling or purpose.

This all seems so elementary—things you probably learned in kindergarten or Sunday school. So, what gets in our way? When we go back to the definition of kindness, caring and compassion, it all starts when we *see* the need or hurt in another. That key word is *see*! I believe that one of the greatest obstacles of fully living Commitment Number One, is that when we get so busy with our lives, we are blinded to the needs of others. If we cannot *see*, we cannot *feel*. If we do not *feel*, we do not *act*, wasting the opportunity to positively impact the life of another.

Several years ago, I had the chance to cross an item on off my bucket list: I went to a week-long, high-performance driving school to learn to operate open-wheel Indy cars. It was one of those experiences I will forever cherish. I learned so much. Some lessons I already knew – like don't hit the wall! But I also learned a key truism that transcended the car lesson and helped me improve my personal and professional life as well. When we were learning to go around the corners of the track, my instructor said, *Remember this: You have to go slow to go fast.* He went on to explain that when you enter the turn (corner), you have to slow the car down to gain control, which will then, ironically, enable you to move through the corner faster by fully accelerating. It saves you time, fuel, and energy. It creates the most efficient momentum. It was a valuable lesson, and I began to consider its relevance to my life. Previously, I had spent my days going full throttle, only to find myself burnt out, and losing control.

Let me ask you, when do your best ideas come to you? I doubt many of you would answer when you are stressed, busy and out of control. Our best ideas, decisions and innovations come to us when our brains are at rest, when we are *moving slowly*. The same is true of our ability to see needs of others, creating opportunity to demonstrate compassion.

APPLICATION and DISCUSSION

- What are the things in your life that get in the way of being the compassionate leader you aspire to be?

- When was the last time that someone genuinely demonstrated compassion to you, and how did it make you feel?

- What impact might a culture of compassion have on an organization, a team, or a family?

COMMITMENT: What is one thing I can do *every day* to be better at Commitment One? Every day, I will demonstrate kindness and caring for all those I interact with?

2
COMMITMENT TWO

We live in an era of declining trust. In the early 1970s, half of Americans said that most people can be trusted. Today that figure is less than a third. A recent Pew Research poll found that trust declines sharply from generation to generation. In 2018, only 29% of Americans over 65 said that most people can't be trusted, while for those aged 18 to 29, fully 60% feel the same way. This same research suggests that one's level of trust erodes with age, which does not bode well for the future, as trusting generations are replaced by mistrustful ones. With this bleak outlook, you may be asking yourself … how do we turn this tide of trust erosion?

Trust is the ultimate result that comes from investing in others. Trust is the glue that holds relationships together. It is not about merely believing in someone, but taking action toward that belief. As a consequence, genuine trust can't be realized until it's extended to someone else. Thus, commitment number two: *Every day*, **I will extend trust even before it is earned and assume positive intent of everyone.**

Wow! That commitment is easy to say, but a different thing altogether to actually do every single day. It runs counter to human nature for most of us. The tricky thing about trust is that it can mean different things to different people. For example, if you were to say to me "I don't trust you," I might easily interpret that as a direct attack on my integrity. But trust can also refer to competency—how well or how quickly you do something. And when the word "trust" is misunderstood, conflict results. Trust is a fickle friend. We all see trust from different perspectives.

Back in the 1980s, the United States was at the twilight of a decades-old Cold War with the Soviet Union. During this time, President Reagan was in constant talks with Soviet General Secretary Mikhail Gorbachev. In 1986, the President's advisor on Russian Affairs, Suzanne Massie, suggested that perhaps Reagan ought to learn a few Russian proverbs. The one he liked best was *"Doveryai no proveryai"* — trust, but verify, an axiom that entered American usage when Reagan began to use it during his interactions. He liked it so much, in fact, that Gorbachev expressed annoyance at the President for using it at every meeting.

Another perspective is that trust is earned only when someone "deserves" it—when you are certain that this person is not going to let you down or fail to help you when you need it. Growing up in Missouri, I would always see the motto on license plates: "Show

Me." The most widely known legend attributes the phrase to Missouri's Congressman, Willard Duncan Vandiver, who served in the United States House of Representatives from 1897 to 1903. While a member of the U.S. House Committee on Naval Affairs, Vandiver attended an 1899 naval banquet in Philadelphia. In a speech there, he declared, *I come from a state that raises corn and cotton and cockleburs and Democrats, and frothy eloquence neither convinces nor satisfies me. I am from Missouri. You have got to show me.*

Trust can never be *earned*; it can only be *given*.

As Everyday Leaders, we have the opportunity to see trust differently. What if we changed our perspective on trust away from the façade we hide behind, or a prize that someone in our lives finally wins, but as a gift that is our obligation as Everyday Leaders to bestow? **Trust can never be earned; it can only be given.**

This is a concept that may be completely backwards to many of us. We may struggle with this concept because it places the responsibility on us as the givers of trust, versus the behaviors of the "earners" of trust.

When we really think about it, we realize how unfair it is, waiting on another to earn trust. When we subscribe to this ideology, we must realize that this means we are, in effect, "keeping score." We have a trust scorecard that only we are aware of. Every time we keep score, we create a winner and a loser. In the game of relationships, this creates a loss for everyone. The reality of a scorecard is that no one is good enough or consistent enough to maintain our high standings. Everyone will fall short from time to time, and this journey has no end. When we change our perspective, we realize that **trust is a choice**—a choice that *we* control.

This line of thinking isn't for those people in your life who will take great advantage of you—or perhaps who already have. It isn't for casual encounters, and it certainly doesn't mean you splash your checking account number across social media platforms. This line of thinking is for people with whom you are in personal relationships, those with whom you wish to have a high degree of mutual trust, and where winning the relationship game is key.

Now, don't get me wrong. I am in no way advocating being gullible or naïve. You shouldn't be a push-over. But neither am I suggesting that living in a constant state of suspicion and distrust is in any way beneficial to our mental health and relationships. We need to consider that trust lies on a continuum. On one extreme of the continuum is mistrust or suspicion. The other end represents blind trust or gullibility.

DISTRUST/ SUSPICION ———————————— BLIND TRUST/ GULLIBILITY

The reality is, is if we live our lives at either end of that continuum, we will constantly see ourselves as the resister, one who has difficulties in our teams and our relationships. I understand that there are several reasons that we lean periodically toward the position of mistrust. We may have learned to be suspicious because of our upbringing, our origin, or maybe our cultural and social conditioning led us to mistrust others. Certainly, what we read or watch can breed more fear than trust, and can work to shut down a naturally trusting heart. We have to find ways sometimes to extend trust to enable us to live in the middle. After studying teams for many years, I've come to realize that most conflict does not arise from trusting each other too *much*, but too *little*.

Trust can be highly influential. Trust is a bit like a spiral. When we trust, and extend trust to others, it can be felt. And when we do extend trust to others, they want to do their very best not to disappoint. They will wish to live up to both, from perspectives of character and competency, and to the expectations that we have when we trust them. But the opposite is also true. When we are distrustful, people can sense that as well. And when that happens, they will rarely live up to the commitments or expectations that we've set. Trust matters.

Let me tell you little story about extending trust

and the impact that it can have on someone else's life. Some time ago, I was standing in my driveway and got an opportunity to speak with a neighbor who was out for a walk. As we got into a discussion on the difficulty of the times that we were in, and on the subject of trust, he told me a story that perfectly exemplifies the power of extending trust.

My neighbor is an accomplished professional in his 50s now, but he told me a story about when he was in high school—a time when he didn't always hang around with some of the best of friends, and didn't always make the best decisions. And he told me about when he and some friends got into trouble for breaking into cars, stealing car stereos or other items of value. As he told me that story, I could see that it wasn't a pleasant time in his life.

The thing you have to understand is that my neighbor is an avid golfer today, just as he was in high school. A second thing you need to understand is that my neighbor and his wife weren't just high school sweethearts—their relationship began in grade school. The story that he told me was about her father, who is actually now his father-in-law. While they were dating in high school, he told me the story of his father-in-law coming to him and saying, *"I know you love to play golf. I own a golf cart rental business, as you know, and anytime that you want to use one of the golf carts, here is a key to my shop. Go in and use the cart. All I ask is that when you're done, if it's an electric cart, plug it back in, or if it's a gas cart, fill it back up with gas. And keep it clean so that it'll be ready when someone comes to use it."* My neighbor said he sheepishly looked at the gentleman, who is now his father-in-law, and said, "You understand that I've been in trouble with the law for stealing. I just wanted to make sure you to know that." And he told me that the gentleman looked down at him, and said, *"Well, I guess I'm just going to have to trust you now, aren't I?"*

And as my neighbor told me that story, I could see the tears form in his eyes. After all this time, it is still that emotional for him. And he said that in that moment, that man changed his identity. That is, he changed the way that my neighbor saw himself—not as a misfit, or a criminal, but actually someone who was worthy of trust.

You can see from that story that extending trust changes lives. What keeps us from doing so? Is it the fear of being let down? Of being burnt? Well, the reality of life is there are those times where we're going to be disappointed when we've extended trust. But I think if you consider it, you'll understand that the benefits of extending trust far outweigh any potential disappointment.

As Everyday Leaders, my challenge to you is to go and positively impact someone's life by extending trust.

APPLICATION and DISCUSSION:

- Are you more inclined to initially distrust others than to trust them? Where do you believe you live on the trust continuum?

- Who was that first person who extended trust to you that you will always remember?

- What keeps us from extending trust to others?

- What can we do EVERY DAY that would make us someone to whom people would want to extend trust?

COMMITMENT: What is one thing I can do EVERY DAY to be better at Commitment Two? EVERY DAY I will extend trust even before it is earned and I always assume positive intent.

3

COMMITMENT THREE

Albert Schweitzer said it best:
"A good example has twice the value of good advice."

American author James Baldwin, noted for his works on personal identity and civil rights, states that *"Children have never been very good at listening to their elders, but they have never failed to imitate them."* Any message can be drowned out by conflicting actions.

If you ask people about their early important influences, most will mention their parents. As a rule, home is where we first experience the shadow concept. Most parents learn quickly that telling their children, "do *as I say, not as I do,*" just isn't a workable concept. Children generally tune out the words and copy the behaviors they see instead. They are expert mimics. If you watch them at play, you can hear and see them mimic the adult behaviors that they've observed. *"Like mother, like daughter"* and *"like father, like son"* are more than mere expressions.

These lines from Dorothy Law Nolte are powerful reminders of our influence:

➢ If children live with criticism, they learn to condemn.

➢ If children live with hostility, they learn to fight.

➢ If children live with ridicule, they learn to be shy.

➢ If children live with shame, they learn to feel guilty.

➢ If children live with tolerance, they learn to be patient.

➢ If children live with encouragement, they learn confidence.

➢ If children live with praise, they learn to appreciate.

➢ If children live with fairness, they learn justice.

➢ If children live with security, they learn to have faith.

➢ If children live with approval, they learn to like themselves.

➢ If children live with acceptance and friendship, they learn to find love in the world.

The role of the leader, at work and at home, requires modeling the desired behavior and letting others see the desired values in action. Henry Wheeler Shaw once said: *"To bring up a child in the way he should go, travel that way yourself once in a while."* To become effective leaders, we must become aware of our shadow and then learn to match our actions with our message.

"ACTIONS SPEAK LOUDER THAN WORDS."
"BE A ROLE MODEL."
"SET A GOOD EXAMPLE."
"WALK THE TALK."
"PRACTICE WHAT YOU PREACH."

These familiar phrases have a common message: What we do is just as important, perhaps even more so, as what we say. The most effective leaders shape the culture of their organizations through a powerful combination of behavior and messaging through which we cast a powerful shadow that influences everyone around us: in the workplace, at home and in the community.

The shadow that great leaders cast extends far beyond their own lives. Mother Teresa devoted her life to serving the impoverished, the orphaned, the disabled and the dying. Missionaries of Charity, the order she founded in Calcutta, now operates 700 missions serving the "poorest of the poor" in 183 countries. Even after her death in 1997, her example continues to inspire people around the world.

But the concept of the shadow of the leader is not limited to world leaders. Each of us casts our own shadow, and in doing so we influence those around us. Consider the business leaders, teachers, parents, friends, peers, coaches, church and community leaders that have been influential in your life. How have their shadows influenced you? More than likely, the strongest shadows were cast by those whose actions reinforced their words.

Whether we choose to believe it or not, we are examples to others around us every day, and I guarantee they are watching. You don't have to be the boss, or a celebrity, or in a position of authority to be the EXAMPLE.

Many of the greatest examples of kindness and compassion come from those in the humblest of roles, on teams, in communities and in families.

Our example matters. We are all striving to create a great culture in our organizations, our teams and our families. Culture is simple. There are two simple truths to remember. First, culture is nothing more than the aggregation of attitudes and behaviors of *any* group of people. And second, and most important, culture is most highly influenced by the behavioral *examples* of its leaders.

We must realize that being an example is a

double-edged sword and can easily cut both ways. In everything we do, we cast a shadow of our behaviors, both good *and bad.*

All of this brings us to Commitment #3 of Everyday Leaders: ***Every day, I will strive to be the example that I want others to follow.***

"*Being the example that I want others to follow*" starts with the example that they see in us. They see our presence. Presence is a word that has multiple meanings. We sometimes refer to being "present" in the moment, but *presence* is a bit different. **It is about how others see us.** It is not often discussed, but is critically important to our example and our "shadow."

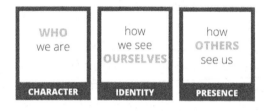

Character is *who* we are. It is our values and our beliefs. Then there is our identity. It is how we see ourselves, and is made up of our successes and failures. It is how we view *ourselves.* Then there is our *presence.*

Our presence is how *others* see us. We all hope that our presence is a clear reflection of our character, yet it is the little things that get in our way. Our body language, the words that we use, our tone, and our communication skills, all make up our presence. Great presence and being a positive example is founded in intentional self-awareness.

Being the example doesn't mean being perfect, it just means getting up every morning and doing our very best, with character and integrity. I would imagine that if I asked you who has had a great impact on your life, and who served as an example to you—maybe someone that you've attempted to emulate—it would probably be their character that stood out to you. It's not the big things we do that create our examples, it's in the little things that we do every single day: being polite, saying "thank you," showing compassion for someone in a moment of need. The little things that we do influence others more than we can ever know.

Many of you are familiar with the Mayo Clinic in Rochester, Minnesota. Among their thousands of employees, one of the most famous among their ranks was Joe Fritch, whom they all referred to as "Joe Clinic." Joe worked there from 1929 to 1954. He wasn't a doctor, an inventor or nurse. Joe was a doorman. Incredibly though, in the time that Joe worked there, he received more notes of appreciation and letters of gratitude than any employee or doctor before or since. Joe was used in the on-boarding process for new employees as the example that they want others to follow. That example wasn't through his skill in opening doors, but in his character and compassion. That is what they want the clinic to stand for. For those decades that Joe worked there, he was well known for his ability to remember patients' names. He was a bit of a cornball, and liked to tell jokes. He had a special affinity for the children of patients, or the children that were coming to seek treatment themselves. You see, Joe was a light in a very dark time in many people's lives. They didn't come to the Mayo Clinic for pleasure. Most of the time it was for treatment, and it all caused serious disruptions in their lives.

Joe helped out by doing little things. He would remember kids on return visits, and know when they were going to show up, often surprising them with little gifts. He would remember all the names of people coming and going and would greet them by name every single morning. And sometimes Joe would even make the kids honorary door people, who would then work with him through the day, opening the doors and greeting people. **Being the example.**

Today, Joe is still the example of the character that they hope all employees will emulate. Well, the other half of that story isn't about the example that Joe created, but was about the example that he was shown.

You see, when Joe was a little boy, his mother was ill. Joe grew up in England, and when he would go to the hospital with his mother, he couldn't always enter the examination rooms, and had to sit out in the hallway, sometimes several days a week. And as Joe was sitting out in the hallway one day, a custodian took notice. He would often stop and carry on a conversation. Then he got to know Joe's name. And then he would intentionally seek out Joe, to the point where a great friendship developed. Joe would become an honorary custodian every once in a while, and walk around the hallways with his friend. That example of character created a legacy in Joe that he went on to exemplify and actually be the standard for others to follow.

Pause for a moment and think about the math behind a few simple gestures. From a simple custodian, caring for a little boy in a hallway, which influenced a man who cared for patients, and is now held in reverence by every employee in one of the most renowned health care organizations in the world today. One person's example, in a moment in time, has directly impacted nearly 100,000 employees caring for 1.3 million patients in 50 states and in 130 countries today.

When you feel like no one is watching and that you can't possibly have an impact, consider the humble, compassionate example of that custodian.

As everyday leaders, we have the opportunity and the obligation to go out and start a legacy simply by being the example that we want others to follow.

APPLICATION AND DISCUSSION

- Tell a story of a time when someone really influenced you by something they did or something they said. Who was it and why was it inspiring to you?

- What are some habits of the good examples you intentionally create every day?

- What are some bad examples you might be unintentionally creating?

- What keeps us from being our best example and casting our best shadow every day?

COMMITMENT: What is one thing I can do EVERY DAY to be better at Commitment Three? *Every day, I will strive to be the example that I want others to follow.*

4

COMMITMENT FOUR

S uccess is an enchanting word. It's the magical stardust we all want to be touched by. It's a goal of its own for many of us—a motivator, a reason to wake up every day with the drive to take on the world.

Luckily, there is no shortage of advice on how you can thrive and prosper. In fact, a simple question to Google, "how to be successful," yields an impressive 891 million results.

Why is success so popular a notion? Simply put, it feels good to be at the top, to see your hard work pay off, to be smiled upon by the good-fate fairy. But every so often, success feels like an elusive dream more than anything real. We talk, read, and write books about it, listen to wise men and women coach us on "how to get there" or on the "habits of the ultra-successful." And yet—it's a tantalizing feeling—you are never completely satisfied with yourself, because there is someone who is always more "successful"— richer, more popular, better looking. So, how can you ever know with certainty that you have finally "made it"? Is there a standard, objective measure of success?

We all define success differently. While some measure success by the size of their bank account, investment portfolio or the square footage of their home, we must ask ourselves, do those things really bring fulfillment and lasting happiness? What defines the indicators of real success? I want you to consider the definition of an Everyday Leader:

An *everyday* leader is a person who **thinks** more about the needs of others than themselves, **speaks** with integrity and **acts** with purpose, consistently, positively impacting the lives of others *every day*!

True success isn't about what we *have*, but what we *give*, and the difference we make in the lives of others. As an Everyday Leader, our job, our obligation, our privilege, is to make those around us successful. I have been the grateful beneficiary of this philosophy from the leaders and mentors with whom I have worked over the years.

I have had the privilege of working with many great teams throughout my career—teams comprised of exceptional leaders from whom I learn every day. The best teams—the ones that far exceed any expectations—are those in which each team member is personally committed to making others successful. It is the collective belief, instilled in each person, that people can only achieve success by elevating those around them. I think about that famous phrase popularized by John F Kennedy— "A rising tide lifts all boats." While this phrase is usually associated with macroeconomic theory, it can play a vital role at work as well. When we strive to make others successful, our examples inspire those around us, who in turn make others around *them* successful. This replication of success is the rising tide in our teams and organizations that elevate everyone.

The impact of this kind of servant leadership is incredibly powerful. Rather than leaders thinking about themselves all the time, they think about others. Rather than worrying about their individual goals or personal agendas, they concern themselves with helping others achieve *theirs*. And rather than trying to outshine the next person in competitive gamesmanship, real leaders take every opportunity to nurture the talents of those around them and turn the spotlight on their team at every opportunity. I don't know about you, but those are the teams I want to be a part of.

Ultimately, the job of successful leaders is to guide a group of people through a difficult objective, and in the process, build up an even larger group of leaders who can do the same. Real success is not measured by amassing material possessions; rather, it is defined by the positive impact we have on others and our ability to cultivate legions of successful leaders.

We've also been talking about the eight commitments that Everyday Leaders make to themselves, and in this chapter we're going to talk about the commitment of proactive accountability; a unique term, and one that isn't often discussed. That commitment is just this: ***Every day*, I will strive to**

make everyone successful by practicing proactive accountability and respect.

We all strive to create cultures of accountability, on our teams, in our organizations and even in our families. But culture is one of those words that often gets stretched, overused and misused. So allow me to build a foundation of truths that I believe regarding culture.

First, the definition of culture is nothing more than the aggregation of attitudes and behaviors of any group of people. When we think about that—when attitudes are positive and aligned and behaviors follow—remarkable things happen. Teams are cohesive. But sometimes when behaviors are negative—potentially even toxic—undesirable behavior is often the result, creating intense conflict.

Second: culture, attitudes, and behaviors, are most influenced, not by motivational posters on the wall, or guest speakers, but by the behavioral examples of you as Everyday Leaders.

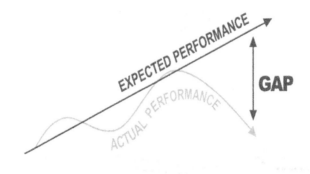

If we think about the term 'accountability' and come back to the culture that we hope to create, most of us have taught (or been taught) the definition of accountability to be an expectation that was set, and a result that was something else, that created a gap —a gap between what I expected and what actually happened. I refer to that as reactive accountability, because when such a gap exists, all we can do is react. We can't go back and undo; all we can do is learn going forward. And there are some good things that come out of reactive accountability.

Let's talk about the Everyday Leader's *proactive* role—to try to illuminate, or at least minimize, that gap. We aren't always going to be able to make it vanish, but I want to talk about what role we play as Everyday Leaders in someone else's accountability, in four steps. Before we get there, however, we need to start with the premise that we want everyone to be successful. When we start with that mindset, we start at step number one. And with every one of these steps, there are traps into which we can fall.

Step number one is that we, as Everyday Leaders, have to be exceptionally clear about our expectations. What we expect. The trap that we can fall into with that, is thinking that a person in a prominent position should simply *know* what's expected of him. That's a trap. As Everyday Leaders, trying to ensure that people are successful, we have the obligation to make sure our expectations are clear, and that we are not merely making assumptions.

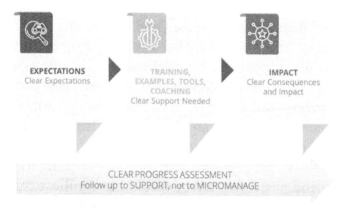

EXPECTATIONS	TRAINING,	IMPACT
Clear Expectations	EXAMPLES, TOOLS,	Clear Consequences
	COACHING	and Impact
	Clear Support Needed	

CLEAR PROGRESS ASSESSMENT
Follow up to SUPPORT, not to MICROMANAGE

Step number two: clarity of investment. With the premise that we want everyone to be successful and that we've been clear about expectations—what do we need to *invest* in that person in order to meet those expectations? Training, coaching, time, tools? Whatever those things are, we want them to be successful. We want them to meet these expectations, and we need to be proactive in thinking about all the things that they need to acquire the capabilities to meet those expectations. It's easy to see the trap that we can fall into. If they need something, they'll come ask us for it. *That's a trap.* Most people would see it as a failure to come and have to ask for help, or time, or learning, or an example, or coaching.

Step number three: we as Everyday Leaders have the obligation to create great clarity around the impact or the 'why' of what we're asking them. What that means is, we all have more things on our plates most days than we have time. There are decisions that we make on a daily basis, prioritizing the things that we're going to do, and maybe the things that aren't going to get done today. We want everyone to be successful, so we have to make our priorities, or impact, clear. For example, we're asking someone to deliver something because that's the first step of a three-step process that someone else is going to pick up. And the ripple effect would be significant if it's not done on time. A level of quality must be achieved because of how something is going to be used. Whatever that is, we have an obligation to help them understand the *impact* and the *'why'* of what we're asking them to do. We know that people engage more when they understand the impact of what we're asking. The trap that we can fall into is, "*Well, I asked* *them to do it—it should be their top priority.*" But as we all know, there are times where we have more things to do than we have time to do them.

Step number four: Going all the way back, we want every single person to be successful, and we've done a wonderful job of setting clear expectations, giving them all the tools and coaching examples that they need, helping them understand the impact and the 'why,' and then we get to step number four, being very clear and intentional with our follow-up, and our progress check. What that really means is, if we want people to be successful, we need to make sure that they are progressing; that things are getting done, and that there are no surprises on the day of delivery. It is a pretty simple trap that we can fall into. Most of us would say, "*I don't want to keep following up with someone on a daily basis to see how it's coming because I don't want to be seen as a micromanager.*" Well, that might be the case if you approached it with the

"Are you done yet?"
"Are you done yet?"
"Are you done yet?"
"Are you done yet?"

In this case, you might be seen as micromanaging. But what if you approached it this way: "*I just wanted to follow-up and see if there's anything more I can do to support you, because I want you to be successful.*" The same result, heard totally different; and you're no longer heard as a micromanager, but you're heard as an Everyday Leader who is supportive and wants to make us successful.

So, remember our premise—we want every single person to be successful—and we do that by being very clear about expectations, giving them the tools and the techniques and the things they need in order to meet those expectations; helping them to understand the clarity of the "why" and the impact of what we're asking them to do; and following up to make sure that we can continue to support them in order for them to succeed.

My challenge to you is this: get out of your own way. Don't fall into these traps. And do your absolute best every single day to make people successful by creating a culture of proactive accountability.

APPLICATION and DISCUSSION:

- How do you feel about the notion *You are responsible for half of everyone else's success? Why do you believe some of us may not feel comfortable taking on that kind of responsibility?*

- Tell a story of a time when you might have fallen into one of the traps in this chapter.

- What are specific instances in your role to which practicing proactive accountability would apply?

- What would a culture of an organization, team, or family look like if we all practiced proactive accountability?

COMMITMENT: What is one thing I can do EVERY DAY to be better at Commitment Four: **EVERY DAY** I will strive to make every person successful through proactive accountability.

5

COMMITMENT FIVE

Several years ago, I had the opportunity to speak at a conference—a milestone event— sharing a message to the largest audience of my career. I honed my message and looked forward to the occasion, for which I had been preparing for months.

The day finally arrived!

As my plane landed and I made my way to my hotel, I felt the same excitement that I'd had as a child stepping out onto a baseball field in a big game.

As I entered this beautiful hotel, I was greeted by the concierge who escorted me to the front desk for check-in. I gave them my name and watched as the desk clerk clicked away, seemingly endlessly, before informing me that I had no room that night. My reservation was for the following week.

I was bewildered. I thought, *how could this have happened TO ME?* All I could think about was the fact that my travel coordinator had made a mistake. I engaged in immediate mental finger pointing. I began to imagine the discussion I was going to have with her, to determine precisely where she had dropped the ball and how she could have failed to pay attention to this critical detail. I planned to clearly explain how this had disrupted my life, making sure to mention the negative impact it had had on a very important trip. But after a few minutes of this finger-pointing exercise, holding someone else responsible, I reevaluated the situation. *"What was my role in creating the problem? My reservation had been on my calendar weeks in advance. Why hadn't I looked at it more closely? What if I hadn't even given her the correct dates?"* I thought.

I then asked myself a question—***how did I let this happen?*** With this simple question, I reframed my experience and acknowledged that, had I acted differently, I likely could have achieved a different outcome. My first reaction wasn't *wrong*, exactly— someone *had* let me down — but I understood that I needed to take personal responsibility for my lack of attention and for *my* role in this misunderstanding.

It seems these days that there are fewer and fewer things that we have control over, but one thing we can *always* control is our attitude in the midst of change and adversity. **We have little control over things that happen to us, but we have *complete* control over how we react to them.**

We have little control over things that happen to us,

but we have *complete* control over how we react to them.

The diagram describes a typical, everyday life. Originally created by Bruce Gordon, President of the NAACP, it describes a ladder having eight rungs in the progression of accountability. The first four rungs indicate a **reactive mindset**, or victim mentality, and the upper four rungs indicate a proactive mindset, or **empowered mentality**.

The red line on this *accountability ladder* represents surprises that happen in our lives. That line can represent so many things, from a flat tire to a new policy or compliance requirement, to a sick family member, or an ever-increasing work load with limited resources. These are all realities of life. They will happen *to us* and we will have no control over them. The only thing we can control is how we react to them.

We have a choice to make each time the red line appears in our lives. We can go down the ladder and take on the victim perspective. We can just wait and see if things change or go away on their own, make up excuses, and ultimately move to denial, blaming everyone else for the things that happen to us.

OR

We can climb the ladder and take on an accountable perspective. We don't have to like the red line, but we do have to accept its reality. Once we do that, we are no longer paralyzed by it. Once we have accepted our situation, we can find solutions and overcome any challenges in front of us ... and there will be plenty.

When we look around, we can recognize those folks who wallow in problems and spend all of their time complaining. We can also recognize those that make the choice to accept the realities and find the courage and determination to overcome. Who do you want to spend your time with?

My grandfather always used to say, there are only two types of people in this world: faucets and drains. You're either the type who that drains us, or the type who fills us up. Those who wallow in misery and problems sap the energy out of us, but those who stay positive and solution-focused fill us up and replenish us. **BE A FAUCET!**

By now, you know that Everyday Leadership has nothing to do with power, hierarchy or authority, or where you sit on an organization chart. It has everything to do with the little opportunities we're presented with every single day, and which can make a substantial difference. That definition of an Everyday Leader is a person that thinks more about the needs of others than themselves, speaks with integrity, acts with purpose, and most importantly —consistently, positively impacts the lives of others every single day. In order to be that kind of leader, we have to hold ourselves accountable—personally accountable to our behaviors.

A few days ago, I heard someone speak on the topic of personal accountability. His name was Dr. John Izzo, and he was telling a story about a company that had just won the designation of the "best place to work in America." This company had just seen fifty-seven consecutive quarters of double-digit profit growth, a 15,000% increase in the employee base in a 10-year period, and a turnover rate 1/5 the industry average. He was intrigued and wanted to understand the secret that set them apart from all of these other companies. He asked the CEO what made them so successful, and his surprising response was *"the power of love."* He handed him a badge and invited him walk around the premises, talking to people—hoping to find the answer he was seeking.

All of them said the same thing—*"the power of love."* As he was walking around, he noticed the same sign hanging everywhere: **100/0**. He asked an employee what it meant, and he responded—*every single one of us takes 100% responsibility for the things that are in our control, with zero excuses.*

This is the basis for Commitment Number Five: ***Every day, I will take 100% responsibility for the things within my control, with 0 excuses.*** Every one of us makes choices every morning when we wake up. I want to talk about five choices that Everyday Leaders make to hold themselves personally accountable.

Choice #1: Be *positive* and *optimistic.* Our attitude is infectious. Our attitude is a decision that each of us make when our feet hit the ground in the morning – It is the most important decision we will make all day. Culture in its simplest form is the aggregation of the attitudes and behaviors of any group of people, teams or families, or organizations. Culture, attitudes and behaviors are most highly influenced by the behavioral examples you set as Everyday Leaders. That means, where our attitude goes, others will follow. The difference between a faucet and a drain is simply *attitude.*

Choice #2: to be accountable rather than feeling victimized. That means trying to figure out what we can do, not just sit around complaining. This goes back to the accountability ladder. Where we sit on that ladder is a *choice*—one that we make every single day.

Choice #3: Focus on what you can do, versus what you cannot. We all have different perspectives about things in life, and in order to hold ourselves accountable, sometimes we have to change our mind's narrative. We do this, not from looking at the things that we *can't* do—the things that hold us back—but by looking for the things within our control. It's much like what we've talked about before: **We see what we look for**. When we look for obstacles and things that get in our way, that's just what we're going to see. But when we look for solutions and opportunities, we will discover those just as often.

Choice #4: Speak up, constructively. We've all been in those meetings where everyone stays silent and you think you all agree, until the meeting ends and then all of a sudden out in the hallway is the sound of the post-meeting murmurs. People team up and complain, or voice their concerns about all that they weren't courageous enough to talk about during the meeting. That is not **100/0** kind of behavior. As Everyday Leaders, we have the opportunity—and the *obligatio*n—to speak up constructively and respectfully to make sure our voices and opinions are heard to those who matter and who can do something about it.

Choice #5: putting the goals of the team

and the organization before any *personal* goals. Understanding the right thing for the group and the department, and the goals we're trying to accomplish, versus the *what's in it for me* attitude. It comes back to one facet of Everyday Leadership: *An Everyday Leader is a person who thinks about the needs of others before themselves.*

These are five choices that every single one of us can make every single day to hold ourselves accountable. Not just sometimes, not just when we feel like it, but 100% of the time. My challenge to you is just that. Every day, practice 100% accountability and zero excuses for that which is within your control.

APPLICATION and DISCUSSION:

- Tell a story of a time when you made a mistake; how did you react to that moment?

- What is one area in your life in which you have the greatest opportunity to focus, to be most impactful as an Everyday Leader?

- When someone gives you feedback, how do you view it (opportunity or criticism) and how do you react?

- What do you believe is one obstacle holding you back right now and what is in your control to overcome it?

COMMITMENT: What is one thing I can do EVERY DAY to be better at Commitment Five: *EVERY DAY, I will take 100% responsibility for the things within my control, with 0 excuses.*

We see what we look for.

6
COMMITMENT SIX

I would imagine that if I asked you to tell me a story of someone who has challenged you in your life, you would tell me of a person who cared about you enough to see your potential, and helped you see that in yourself.

Recall the definition of an Everyday Leader: An **EVERYDAY** leader is a person who *THINKS* more about the needs of others than themselves, *SPEAKS* with integrity and *ACTS* with purpose, consistently, positively impacting the lives of others **EVERY DAY!**

The last statement of that definition could not be more apropos for this chapter. We've been walking through the eight commitments of Everyday Leaders, and now we're going to discuss commitment six: *Every day, I will seek and develop potential in others, including myself.*

All of us have been influenced by leaders, from mentors and coaches to teachers and politicians ... and the reality is that all great leaders out there have, at one time, had leaders who have been examples to them—those who have been able to develop potential in them that they may not have been able to see themselves. And I think that's one of the principles that we all must understand: **We see what we look for**.

That principle reminds me of a story that I once heard about one of the greatest violinists of our time, Joshua Bell. In January 2007, Joshua Bell decided to conduct a social experiment. One morning, he put on a t-shirt and baseball cap and posed as a street musician in a subway in Washington, D.C. The interesting thing about this social experiment was that just the previous night, Joshua Bell had performed at the Library of Congress where tickets to attend started at $200.

With a hidden camera in place, Joshua Bell walked into the subway station that morning to perform and to see if anybody would notice him. That camera documented his 43-minute performance. At 7:51 a.m. on Friday, January 12, Joshua Bell opened up his violin case, and pulled out his 1713 Stradivarius violin, worth $3.5 million dollars. He then began his performance with Bach's 14-minute Partita No. 2 in D-minor, one of the greatest musical compositions ever written, being played on one of the greatest instruments ever made. What happened next was truly incredible.

Nearly three minutes went by before anyone even noticed Joshua Bell. 63 people had walked right by Joshua when one gentleman slowed for just a moment, turned his head, noticed that someone was there, and then …. just kept walking. A half a minute later, Bell actually got his first donation. A woman walking by tossed a dollar into his case and slinked off. It was not until six minutes into his performance that someone even stopped to listen to him. 43 minutes into his performance, nearly 1100 people walked past this virtuoso-turned-busker. No more than a handful even stopped to notice him. He ended up receiving just over $32 in donations. $20 of that amount came from one person. Everyone was too busy to notice the majesty of the performance that was directly in front of them.

I think that story is actually a metaphor for many of us. We get so busy in our hustle and bustle that we miss the shock and awe—we fail to see the majesty of the potential in others. I think there are a couple of things that we can do to sharpen our perspective and maybe *see* what we *look* for.

In a brief essay that appeared circa 1925, poet Katharine Lee Bates described how during a trip to Pikes Peak in 1893, she was inspired to write "America the Beautiful," the poem that would later become one of the nation's best-loved patriotic songs. Bates was a professor at Wellesley and had traveled west to teach a summer course in Colorado Springs. Bates and the other professors decided to "celebrate the close of the session with a merry expedition to the top of Pikes Peak." They made the ascent by prairie wagon. At the top, Bates later wrote, she was inspired by "*the sea-like expanse of fertile country . . . under those ample skies,*" and "*the opening lines of the hymn floated into my mind."* Those opening lines—*"O beautiful for spacious skies / For amber waves of grain / For purple mountain majesties / Above the fruited plain!"*—would eventually become the lyrics of one of the best-known songs in American history. As she sat at the top of Pikes Peak, she saw majesty.

Decades after Katherine Bates' trek to the top of that mountain, I recall visiting friends in Colorado Springs. One morning as the sun came up, I glanced out of their window and saw Pikes Peak in all its glory. I turned to my friends and commented what a blessing it must be to awaken to that splendor every morning. They said, *"in the rush to get out of the door in the morning we rarely take time to look."*

This raises the question, how do you *"take time to look"*? What does that mean in our lives? How do we get out of our own way to slow down, to see a different view – potential in others and ourselves.

In order to see potential, we have to *look* in three ways:

First, we must understand that we find potential in passion. If we think about that, some of the things that we are best at are the things that we're most passionate about. How many times have you seen someone in a role in which they may be mediocre, or sub-optimal? Yet they change roles, maybe even in the same organization, and get into a position for which they have great passion. And all of a sudden, they thrive. The organization's the same, the person is the same, but now the potential is seen because of the passion. So how do we find that in others? It is all about getting to know people, understanding them, not for the role that they play, but for the people that they are. When we understand their passions, we understand the direction toward their greatest potential.

I heard a story about an engineer in a company. On a scale a 1-10, he was, at best, a 6. He was passed over year after year for opportunities for promotion and advancement in the engineering department. The common theme was that *"he just wasn't ready yet."* Then an opportunity became available for a management position in customer service and he applied. During his interview there was a spark in his eye and passion in his voice. The company decided to give him a chance. Over the next twelve months, he thrived. He not only improved, but was nominated for team member of the year. How does someone go from a 6 to a 10 in a matter of months? When he was asked that very question he said "*I was an engineer because my grandfather was an engineer, my father was an engineer, and I assumed I was supposed to be an engineer. I found my passion. I now love what I do.*"

Second, we have to remember that we can't judge potential on past performance. So many times, we look at someone and see the things that they have done in the past, and use that to determine their potential. It's the perspective that we have, or maybe the lenses that we look through. To be able to truly develop the full potential in others, we have to see what they *can be*, not what they *have been*. We have to see what they can *achieve*, not what they have *done* or where they have fallen short. And it's interesting because I think these statements hold true not only for seeking and understanding the potential in others, but also in our *own* potential. So many times, our identity, our perspective, the lens that we look through—even when we look at ourselves—is based upon our past versus our passion and our future.

Sir Edmund Hillary was born in 1919 and grew up in Auckland, New Zealand, where he became interested in mountain climbing. Although he made his living as a beekeeper, he climbed mountains in New Zealand, the Alps, and ultimately, in the Himalayas, climbing 11 different peaks, each over 20,000 feet in height. At age 33, Hillary was ready to tackle the world's highest peak—Mount Everest.

As he first stood at the base of Everest, looking up at the awe-inspiring view, contemplating the great task that lay ahead of him and his team, he said, *"It is not the mountain that we conquer, but ourselves."*

Hillary made several unsuccessful attempts at scaling Mount Everest before ultimately succeeding. After one attempt, he stood at the base of the giant mountain and shook his fist at it. *"I'll defeat you yet,"* he said defiantly, *"because you're as big as you're going to get—but I'm still growing."* Every time Hillary climbed, he failed. And every time he failed, he learned. And every time he learned, he grew and tried again. And one day he no longer failed.

Failure does not shape you; the way you respond to failure shapes you.

How do you define failure? Basketball player Michael Jordan puts it this way: "*I've missed over 9000 shots in my career, have been beaten in 300 games, been entrusted with the last-second winning shot 26 times and missed. I've failed again, and again, and again, and that is why I succeeded.*" If Jordan had blamed himself after every missed shot and gotten hung up on his failures, would he have become the icon that he is today?

Failure is not an end—quite the opposite. Each failure is a step we take on the path to success. This a perspective that may be very difficult for us to accept. If you're a perfectionist or accept defeat the minute you stumble, please take note: **Failure is our best teacher.** "*An example is better than precept,*" as the old proverb goes. If you've made a mistake on the road to success, you can always learn from it and use what you've learned along the way.

What we need to do is to accept this simple realization: We have to get out of our own way. Each time we stumble, think of it as a blessing and not a curse. The worst thing we can do is be so scared of what is in front of us that we never even try.

IT IS NOT THE MOUNTAIN THAT WE CONQUER, BUT OURSELVES.

Finally, as Everyday Leaders, we have the obligation to nudge, encourage and challenge others to be their very best. Many people are like butterflies. Butterflies are blessed with great vision. They have compound eyes (multiple lenses), and possess the rare ability to see in many directions at once. In spite of this, butterflies do not have the ability to look backwards. They cannot see their own beauty. They have no idea that they are one of the most beautiful creatures on earth. As Everyday Leaders, we have the obligation to help others find their beauty, value, and potential. That means that we need to nudge others, encourage them, and challenge them to be their very best. We have to help them see the beauty that they cannot see on their own. This also means that we need to employ that same thought process for ourselves. If we are like that butterfly, we need to find a mirror and recognize our own beauty.

As Everyday Leaders, one of the greatest gifts that we can give to another is helping them find, discover and develop their potential. My challenge for you is just this—know what you are looking for. Don't miss majesty. Find the potential in yourselves—and others—every single day.

APPLICATION and DISCUSSION:

- What gets in our way of discovering and developing potential? In others? In ourselves?

- Who was someone in your life that encouraged you to take on a new challenge and who saw great potential in you?

- What is your driving passion?

- What is the moment in your life that you are most proud of and why?

COMMITMENT: What is one thing I can do EVERY DAY to be better at Commitment Six? *Every day, I will seek and develop potential in others, including myself.*

7
COMMITMENT SEVEN

several words or phrases in the English language have significant potential impact—words like *sorry, trust, thank-you,* and **why**. When we take the time to figure out **why**, it brings clarity, it eliminates assumptions, it builds relationship and creates engagement. It is a very powerful word when we slow down long enough to use it.

The commitment we are going to focus on in this chapter is about our **whys**. **Every day, I will seek to achieve extraordinary results by focusing on our whys.** That seems like such an interesting and simple concept—and it is—to write down or to say—but, for some reason, it is always a difficult concept on which to follow through.

The best way for me to explain the power of **why** is to relate a little story a professor once told me about a homework assignment that he had given. It was February 1989, Boston, Massachusetts. Four students walked into a local Kinkos to conduct a case study. For those of you who don't remember the dark ages of 1989, people would often go to the neighborhood Kinkos to make copies. You would walk up to the counter, get your copy card, and then stand in what was normally a very long line —waiting your turn at the machines. You took that card and plugged it into the copy machine, made your copies, took the card out, and finally went back up to the counter to pay. It wasn't a particularly enjoyable experience—certainly not something that people did for recreation—it was done strictly out of necessity.

These four students on that night elected one of the four to be the spokesperson for the group. The social experiment that they conducted was simply this: In 10-minute intervals, approach the first person in line and say, *"Can I go next?"* Without any other explanation. What do you think their success rate was?

It was actually much higher than I thought it would be— 11%.

Eleven percent of some very conflict-adverse people who gave up their place in line. As the night went on, and they let the line cycle through a few times, they altered their method. The same person would now once again approach the first person in line and say, *"Can I go next, because..."* And followed up with anything after that: *"I'm double parked." "I need to get home let my dog out." "My ice cream is melting."* The statement after the *because* didn't matter.

They simply provided a *reason*. Miraculously, their

success rate jumped from 11% to 82%. And all because of **one** word.

Because.

That was the only variable. The same person was asking the question, in the same Kinkos, on the same night. But when people understood the *why*—the success rate changed.

If you think about it, the same little exercise is relevant in our teams today. When we don't understand the **why**, we're less likely to engage—less convinced that it makes sense.

Let's suppose you get asked to work an extra shift. Your attitude without the *why* might be: *That's unfair. I'm doing everything around here, no one else is pulling their weight. Why can't someone else do that?* And then you learn that that shift that you're taking is for a person who needs to stay home that week with their sick, elderly mother.

The *why*.

It changes the way that we see our own situations. It impacts our engagement and helps us to understand.

Our acceptance hinges less on whether or not we approve of the *why*; and more on just understanding what the reason is, and that it seems logical to us. When our sense of fairness is placated, we're more likely to engage and to be empowered. But actually, the converse is also true. When we don't understand the *why*, or we don't explain the *why* to others, it is more likely that they will become disengaged—

even disgruntled—in performing whatever task they have, or moving in the direction that they're being asked to take.

To help you better understand this concept of **why**, let me explain it from three perspectives—the **big** whys, the **little** whys, and the **my** whys.

I get the opportunity to visit many different organizations and hear things quite frequently like:

"I don't know where we're going as an organization"
"I don't know what our future looks like" or
"I don't know what we're really trying to accomplish here."

We as Everyday Leaders have the obligation to seek to understand the big, strategic **whys** of our teams and our organizations, and also to communicate those to others. When we understand the bigger picture, it changes the perspective of what is asked of us.

On July 20, 1969, Neil Armstrong took the "one giant leap for mankind" on the occasion of the first moon landing. It was the final step of a process that began when one leader with a bold idea lit the collective imagination of a 400,000-person organization — NASA.

According to popular legend, during a tour of NASA headquarters in 1961, John F. Kennedy encountered a janitor mopping the floors.

"Why are you working so late?" Kennedy asked. *"Mr.*

President," the janitor responded, "*I'm helping put a man on the moon.*"

Every employee from the astronauts and engineers to the secretaries and interns were singularly focused on this **big why**.

But just as important, if not more so, are those every day **little whys**. We all get asked to complete tasks, generate reports, do activities, and we ask the same of others. When we take time to explain the **why** behind it—**why** it needs to be done by Friday, or **why** this is a higher priority, we and others are more likely to engage, embrace and accomplish those tasks.

The third perspective is **my why**. This **why** is about the impact we have on those we serve. This **why** inspires us. It provides a clear answer to the questions, "*Why do I get out of bed every morning?*" "*What impact do I make?*" "*Why do I do what I do?*"

Many, however, tend to believe that money and fame are their **whys**—that monetary success and popularity are their true motivations—these momentary diversions that pacify us in our journey to have impact and to be significant. The real significance comes from our *impact*, not our *income*.

Our passion and purpose release our greatest potential. I'm reminded of a quote from Martin Luther King, "*If a man is called to be a street sweeper, he should sweep streets even as Michelangelo painted, or Beethoven composed music or Shakespeare wrote poetry. He should sweep streets so well that all the hosts of heaven and earth will pause to say, 'Here lived a great street sweeper who did his job well."*

We have to understand that every job performed with distinction is honorable, and it is in that honor, we live out the definition of Everyday Leadership: **EVERYDAY** leaders are those who **THINK** more about the needs of others than themselves, **SPEAK** with integrity and **ACT** with purpose, consistently, positively impacting the lives of others **EVERY DAY!**

That is a life worth living.

Many things can get in our way of this simple concept of the *why*. We get so busy that we don't have time to explain the *why*, or maybe the mental trap we fall into is, *I shouldn't **have** to explain the **why**, they should just do as they're asked.* We have to realize that those are traps. And we have to understand that there is so much more that can be accomplished with the slightest effort ... of explaining *why*.

My challenge to you is just this: Embrace this simple concept of the *why*. And do as we talk about in the definition of Everyday Leadership: Act with purpose in explaining—and doing—our *whys* every single day.

APPLICATION and DISCUSSION

- **BIG WHY** – Is there a big why you don't understand? What is it? How do you seek out the why?

- **LITTLE WHY** – Describe a time when someone explained the why behind a task. Maybe someone told you why what you did mattered. How did it make you feel? How did it impact your engagement?

- **MY WHY** - So how do we put this into action? How do we transition from occupation to vocation, from success to significance? Take a few minutes, look back over your career and your life and look for common threads:
  - the reason you were drawn to the jobs you held
  - your most rewarding work accomplishments
  - compliments colleagues gave you about your work
  - circumstances that made you feel productive
  - what you look forward to when you wake up in the morning
  - what has made you feel valuable

Once you've made a list, read each statement and ask yourself, "Why?" That simple question will get you to delve deeper, so you can discover your own *why*. Once discovered, pursue it with passion EVERY DAY.

COMMITMENT: What is one thing I can do EVERY DAY to be better at Commitment Seven? **Every day, I will seek to achieve extraordinary results by focusing on our *whys*.**

8

COMMITMENT EIGHT

G ratitude is a topic that we were taught in kindergarten—be polite, show appreciation, and say 'thank you.' This is not a new concept, but maybe one that is underappreciated and sometimes forgotten altogether.

In physics, the theory of perpetual motion is defined as the motion of a body or object that continues forever. I wonder ... what if we thought of gratitude and appreciation in the same way—not as intentional acts or planned deeds—but as *movement*? What if every act of gratitude leads to another ... in perpetuity? One kind word leads to another, and another. We don't always fully realize just how powerful we are. We all have the ability to impact the lives of others with a few simple words and a small gesture of gratitude.

As Everyday Leaders, we need to follow commitment number eight: ***Every day*, I will appreciate all that I have and show gratitude to all.**

As I think about this topic of gratitude, it reminds me of a study that I read that occurred a couple of years ago at Indiana University. A couple of professors got a group of 300 students together, all of whom were currently undergoing mental health counseling related to depression and anxiety. These two professors divided the 300 participants into three distinct groups, with each assigned different activities.

The first group was asked to write a letter of appreciation and gratitude, once a week, to someone who had, at one time, impacted their lives. Then they were to mail that letter—once a week, for three weeks.

The second study group was asked, also once a week for three weeks, to sit down and explore some thoughts that they had about negative experiences they'd had, and document each one—once a week, for three weeks.

The third group was asked to do nothing at all. And it was very interesting because all of these 300 people continued with counseling. After four weeks, and again at 12 weeks, these professors analyzed the results. What they found was that the mental health of those students who had engaged in expressing gratitude, had exponentially improved relative to the other two samplings. The third group, that did nothing at all, made some slight progress through counseling, but the second group, that spent their time focusing on negative experiences in their lives, actually experienced reversals related to their counseling and their mental health.

It kind of goes to show that quantifiably

demonstrating gratitude actually has a positive effect on both our physical and mental health. We all know that it's the right thing to do, but there are many reasons that gratitude matters. Let's explore three of them.

1. Gratitude is a choice—actively choose it every day.

It astounds me how Christmas decorations begin appearing on the store shelves even before the Halloween candy goes on sale. Toy sales appear on television before the first fall leaves turn red. Don't get me wrong—I am a fan of Christmas and all that it stands for—but one cause of concern is that the Thanksgiving season gets lost in the shuffle.

While controversy surrounds many of the details of the first Thanksgiving and the origin of many of its traditions, there is one constant—the Thanksgiving holiday is a time in which we pause to reflect the blessings we have been given, and all of those things for which we are thankful. We can all use a time to allow our everyday tasks and struggles to fade away, as we focus on our blessings. Can you imagine experiencing that kind of blessing *every day*? That is only possible when we develop the habit of an attitude of gratitude. These are lessons that we learned in kindergarten as the "right" thing to do.

I believe that **we see what we look for.** To cultivate an attitude of gratitude, we must look for things to appreciate daily and develop the habit of *active* gratitude. This is different from *reactive* gratitude, where you wait for something to happen before you express appreciation. With active gratitude, you consciously look for ways to be grateful. Expressing gratitude becomes a choice. When you express gratitude daily, the things and people you appreciate increase in value. We also start to discover more things to be grateful for, changing our perspective, and creating a mindset of appreciation, positivity and contentment. Being more grateful more often makes us happier and more optimistic.

That's Fine, You Say .... But How?

You've probably thought that being thankful was a good thing, or even the morally responsible position. Hopefully, you see it can be even more powerful than simply doing *the right thing*.

Gratitude is an attitude. Gratitude is a choice. And gratitude is a habit. When we consciously and **actively** practice being grateful for the people, situations, and resources around us, we begin to develop better relationships and achieve superior results. The habit will be strengthened as you make the choice *every day*.

2. Gratitude and appreciation creates resilience and pulls us together.

I live in Minnesota, and the fall is a magical and beautiful time. The temperatures begin to drop, the maple trees turn from green to a brilliant red, and apple orchards are filled with families enjoying this beautiful time of year. It is spectacular, as well as a clear indication that winter is just around the corner. One tell-tale sign is the light blue, cloudless skies filled with geese heading south for the winter. As the sun sets in October, the silence of falling leaves is broken by the honking of Canadian geese on the long journey to their warm, winter home. It is a beautiful and curious sight to watch these birds flying in perfect formation. Interestingly enough, I believe there is much we can learn from geese. When you see geese heading south for the winter, flying in that predictable "V" formation, you might consider what science has discovered about their flight. As each bird flaps its wings, it creates an uplift for the bird immediately following. By flying in a V formation, the entire flock can travel at least 71% farther than if each bird flew on its own. People who share a common direction and sense of community can get where they are going more quickly and easily, because they are traveling on the "uplift" of another.

When a goose falls out of formation, it suddenly feels the drag and resistance of trying to go it alone.

It quickly returns to formation to take advantage of the lifting power of the bird in front. **There is a lot we can learn from geese about being *one team*, and the power of lifting each other up. We can go further together.**

Geese believe in structure, but not bureaucracy. Geese take turns leading and performing the difficult tasks. The "lead" goose at the tip of the V formation carries the heaviest load, working to deflect the headwinds and to be the first point of lift for the others. The typical, migratory journey of Canadian geese is 4000 miles, averaging 1550 miles per day. It only stands to reason that no one bird can take the point position for the entire journey. When the lead goose gets tired, it rotates back in the formation and another goose moves ahead to fly point. **There is a lot we can learn from geese about sharing the load to make sure no one individual needs to carry the entire load for others, which inevitably creates burnout and exhaustion.**

Geese understand the need for encouragement, gratitude and appreciation. They honk from behind to encourage those up front to maintain their speed, and through the headwinds, they manage to persevere. **There is a lot we can learn from geese— that a kind and encouraging word goes a long way.**

Finally, when a goose becomes ill and falls out— or is wounded from a hunter's gun—two other geese follow it down to offer aid and protection. They stay until the fallen goose is able to fly or until it dies, and only then do they launch out on their own, or with another formation, to catch up with their group. **There is a lot we can learn from geese about how we stick together and support each other, even in the most difficult of times.**

"If you want to go fast, go alone; if you want to go far, go together."
- African Proverb

3. Gratitude and appreciation bring out our best.

Think about someone in your life who frequently shows you gratitude and appreciation. They tell you you're doing a good job, they thank you, they may even use the words "I appreciate you." How does that make you feel about them? How does it make you see them differently? In most cases, if we thought about it long enough, we would know that it actually improves our relationships with them. It makes us want to perform for them, not wishing to let them down.

I recently visited a historic battleship while on a family vacation. As we were leaving the tour, we saw a number of military artifacts on display, including a wall of military awards, metals and ribbons.

The wall inspires a sense of awe as one recognizes the sheer scope and magnitude embodied by such displays. A quotation at the top of the wall was one that should inspire every leader at every level in every organization. This tough, driven leader who is famous for his passion for winning and his military prowess was none other than ... Napoleon Bonaparte:

> *"It is amazing what a man will do for a piece of colored ribbon."*

One might be tempted to interpret the quote through a lens of cynicism and ridicule. Does this not reinforce the notion that people can be manipulated into committing atrocities for the sake of someone's limitless ambition?

I believe there is a different perspective.

Napoleon was sharing a message that every leader should embrace—no one has ever received too much legitimate appreciation and recognition for their honest efforts and results. It doesn't matter how much you think you may give others recognition, there is always room for more as long as it is sincere and that it stands for something important. Psychologically, it is essential that such accolades have intrinsic value.

The secret to effective recognition isn't about objects. It is about meaning and relevance and connection. Make your sincere recognition stand for something important. Show people how their hard work and great results advance the cause.

We all know that gratitude and appreciation are the right things to do. But I think there are several things that sometimes get in our way, or allow us to get in our own way. We get busy, or we wait too long. We believe that if we celebrate gratitude too much, that it becomes commonplace and people just get complacent, or lazy. We have to realize that those are obstacles to be overcome. My challenge to you as Everyday Leaders, is to go out and appreciate all the things that you have, and demonstrate gratitude to others every single day. Make it a habit.

APPLICATION and DISCUSSION:

- The benefits of active gratitude are obvious, so what keeps us from practicing it every day?

- Think of a time when you felt re-energized because someone showed you gratitude. Describe it.

- What does real, genuine and heartfelt gratitude look like?

- How do you think you can change a habit of aspiration to an attitude of gratitude?

COMMITMENT: What is one thing I can do EVERY DAY to be better at Commitment Seven? *Every day*, I **will appreciate all that I have and show gratitude to all.**

9

CONCLUSION

Being an Everyday Leader seems so simple, but what gets in our way? **BUSYNESS.**

Everyone wants to feel valuable and worthwhile, so we have to ask ourselves, where does our greatest value come from? Many of us believe that our importance comes from our busyness. Being busy is often seen as a badge of honor and a marker of self-worth, with a lack of leisure time indicative of status. However, over-scheduling yourself can negatively affect your emotional and physical health, as well as your ability to be the person you aspire to be.

Research suggests that an individual's perceived level of busyness may be heavily connected to their self-worth, as well as how others view their status. Individuals who are busy by choice may feel needed, in demand, and important, thus elevating their feelings of self-worth. This is a lie we tell ourselves and a trap that we can fall into. The goal is to be impactful, not busy. Consider again the definition of an Everyday Leader:

An **EVERYDAY** leader is a person who *THINKS*

more about the needs of others than themselves, **SPEAKS** with integrity, and **ACTS** with purpose, consistently, positively impacting the lives of others **EVERY DAY!**

There is nothing in that definition about being busy. We need to reframe the way we see our significance.

Busyness is the greatest enemy of Everyday Leadership.

I recently performed my own little social experiment. Over the course of a week, I asked 37 people the same simple question, *How are you doing?* The results amazed me. Over 80% responded with the same answer: *busy.* Then I realized that I was probably just as guilty, and wondered how many times I had responded the same way.

Think about the impact of busyness of each of our commitments:

1. EVERY DAY, I will demonstrate **kindness and caring** for all with whom I interact.

Whenever we sympathize with others, we have an opportunity to demonstrate compassion, but when we are busy, we might be blinded to the needs of others, never seeing the opportunity to impact a life with a small act of caring and kindness.

2. EVERY DAY, I will **extend trust** even before it is earned and assume positive intent of everyone.

In order to extend trust, we have to know someone both from a character and competency perspective. We only reach that level of familiarity when we slow down to get to know someone.

3. EVERY DAY, I will **be the example** that I want others to follow.

Being such an example takes great intentionality. Intentionality takes time and gets lost in the busyness of life.

4. EVERY DAY, I will strive to make every person successful through **proactive accountability.**

Owning the success of others takes time and intentionality. We have to slow down to set clear expectations, equip everyone for success, explain the purpose and continuously follow up. Busyness can get in the way of helping others find success.

5. EVERY DAY, I will take **100% responsibility** of things within my control with 0 excuses.

Busyness, distraction and too much to do can quickly become an excuse for holding ourselves accountable.

6. EVERY DAY, I will seek to **discover and develop potential** in everyone, including myself.

We can't see the potential and greatness in others if we are too busy and distracted.

7. EVERY DAY, I will work for extraordinary results by focusing on our **WHY.**

Slowing down to explain the why takes time, and when we are too busy, we can easily see it as unnecessary and without value.

8. EVERY DAY, I will appreciate everything that I have and show **gratitude** to all.

When we're very busy and distracted, we are blinded to those around us. When we can't see them, we can't appreciate them. Slow down to find gratitude.

Once we overcome busyness, we must create awareness. We see what we look for. **We are most significance in our intention to be impactful.**

It's funny how some of our greatest life lessons happen in the most humble and simple of moments. I vividly remember a summer evening when I was 10 years old. My dad and I were driving home from one of my baseball games. It was an away game, so we found a small town in the middle of Missouri to stop and get a quick bite to eat. As we began to walk into the restaurant, we both noticed a boy sitting out front.

The boy—who seemed to be about my age at the time—was filthy and unkempt. My dad walked over to him, took in the situation for a moment, said *hi there, son,* and then asked if he was hungry. The young boy answered with a quiet, but emphatic *yes.*

As we got inside, my father looked at the boy and told him that he could order whatever he wanted. When the food was ready, the boy nervously sat down with us to eat. As we sat there, the young boy, named Tom, told us that his father was out of work, money was tight and that he hadn't eaten all day. As Tom and I sat there talking about the stuff 10-year-olds talk about—baseball and 10-year-old girls—my father excused himself from the table. When he returned, he was carrying a large bagful of sandwiches and told the young boy to take them home. Tom gratefully looked up and asked, *really??* My dad, in his gentle voice replied, *really.*

We said goodbye to Tom and got back in the car. Just as my father reached for the key in the ignition, he turned to me and said, *never miss an opportunity to help someone in need. Always do what you can.* My father was not a man of means, but he was clearly a man of kindness.

I do not doubt that that moment had a profound impact on Tom's life. I hope that it impacted him for a long time, and helped to lift him up. I *hope* these things. Of course, I have no way of knowing about the real impact that it had on his life—but I can tell you that it had an impact on *my* life. My father was not a man of authority or influence, but he was an Everyday Leader, and *that* moment, on *that* night, he inspired me to do my best to help others however I can.

Daily life can be difficult for everyone, and it takes hard work, but it only takes a small gesture to touch another human being. You are the only person that you can control, so when you see an opportunity to offer something, take it.

Whether you have the money, the time or the energy, there is always a way to help someone who really needs it. Take in your surroundings. See the things, people, and feelings that might be hiding in the shadows.

No one can do *everything*, but *everyone* can do *something*. Hopefully, we can all offer a small gift to someone who might need it, whether that be emotional or physical. You may not think that your own actions could impact someone so profoundly, but we never know what someone may be going through at any moment and what a blessing we can be to them.

One of the realities of being an Everyday Leader is the fact that we will never be perfect. When we try to be perfect every day, we will spend our lives in a perpetual state of disappointment. Perfection is the enemy. Progress is the goal.

- Progress is fluid and open. Perfection is rigid and inflexible.
- Perfection is exhausting. Progress is invigorating.
- Perfection wears a mask. Progress is transparent.
- Perfection is endless because you never get there. Progress is endless because you're *always* there.
- Perfection focuses on what's not working, the flaws, the "not-enoughs," the old paradigms. Progress looks at what is working, the improvements, the discoveries, the "aha" moments that come from the realization of looking at things in a new way.

There's beauty in progress. There's simplicity.

My challenge to you is to wake up every morning,

and as your feet hit the floor, commit to do your very best.

COMMIT TO BEING AN EVERYDAY LEADER.

Better every day...

... Impactful every moment...

... In the littlest of things we do.

ABOUT THE AUTHOR

K ent Myers is an author, educator, speaker and consultant who has the opportunity to spend many of his days inspiring executive teams to be their very best and build sustainable cultures of which people are proud to be a part. While Kent has an extensive background in education, he claims that the most significant source of content and encouragement for his lectures and books are in the everyday leadership he sees in everyday people all around us. He believes that we see what we look for and is blessed to spend his days looking for caring, kindness, honesty, and potential in others. He is passionate about helping every person see the power, influence and impact they have in the little things they do every day.

Made in the USA
Coppell, TX
27 January 2023

11751447R00056